T0401015

THE CLIMATE CRISIS IN
THE OHIO VALLEY

by Barbara Lowell

FOCUS
READERS®

NAVIGATOR

WWW.FOCUSREADERS.COM

Focus Readers is distributed by North Star Editions:
sales@northstareditions.com | 888-417-0195

Produced for Focus Readers by Red Line Editorial.

Content Consultant: Donald J. Wuebbles, PhD, Harry E. Preble Emeritus Professor of Atmospheric Sciences, University of Illinois

Photographs ©: Ryan C. Hermens/Lexington Herald-Leader/AP Images, cover, 1, 4–5; Brynn Anderson/AP Images, 7; Shutterstock Images, 8–9, 14–15, 21, 22–23, 25; Red Line Editorial, 10; Amanda Haverstick/The News Dispatch/AP Images, 13; Steve Helber/AP Images, 17; Jeff Roberson/AP Images, 19; Riding Metaphor/Alamy, 27; CN Mages/Alamy, 29

Library of Congress Cataloging-in-Publication Data
Names: Lowell, Barbara, author.
Title: The climate crisis in the Ohio Valley / by Barbara Lowell.
Description: Lake Elmo, MN : Focus Readers, [2024] | Series: The climate
   crisis in America | Includes index. | Audience: Grades 4-6
Identifiers: LCCN 2023002940 (print) | LCCN 2023002941 (ebook) | ISBN
   9781637396339 (hardcover) | ISBN 9781637396902 (paperback) | ISBN
   9781637397985 (pdf) | ISBN 9781637397473 (ebook)
Subjects: LCSH: Endangered ecosystems--Ohio River Valley--Juvenile
   literature. | Biodiversity--Climatic factors--Ohio River
   Valley--Juvenile literature.
Classification: LCC QH76.5.O38 L69 2024 (print) | LCC QH76.5.O38 (ebook)
   | DDC 577.27--dc23/eng/20230125
LC record available at https://lccn.loc.gov/2023002940
LC ebook record available at https://lccn.loc.gov/2023002941

Printed in the United States of America
Mankato, MN
082023

ABOUT THE AUTHOR

Barbara Lowell is an award-winning author of nonfiction picture books, early readers, and educational chapter books. She lives in Broken Arrow, Oklahoma.

TABLE OF CONTENTS

CHAPTER 1

KENTUCKY FLOODS

Powerful thunderstorms rolled into eastern Kentucky on July 25, 2022. That night was the beginning of record flooding. The storms and floods damaged buildings. They washed away homes and cars. Rain fell for several days. Some areas received 16 inches (41 cm) of rain.

A building in Lost Creek, Kentucky, is destroyed after powerful floods in July 2022.

In Hazard, Kentucky, 9 inches (23 cm) fell in 12 hours.

Knott County had three **flash flood** emergencies. People living along Troublesome Creek had never seen such intense rainfall. The creek rose quickly. It crashed over its banks. The water destroyed everything people owned.

The flooding continued. Small streams and creeks poured into a river. In one area, a **stream gauge** recorded the river at 21 feet (6.4 m) above **flood stage**. Then, the gauge broke. So did the record of 14.7 feet (4.5 m) above flood stage.

Boats searched for people trapped by rising water. Helicopters performed

The 2022 floods in Kentucky caused serious damage that lasted long after water levels had dropped.

600 rescues. Even so, 39 people died. **Climate change** is making these kinds of storms more common. The climate crisis is leading to more and more intense storms with heavy rainfall in certain areas.

CHAPTER 2

OHIO VALLEY CLIMATE

Weather involves conditions at one place and time. It describes temperature, **precipitation**, and many other things. Climate is also about those conditions. However, climate describes an area's long-term weather patterns.

The Ohio Valley is the area that borders the Ohio River. It also includes areas with

The Ohio River flows along the borders of several states, including Ohio, West Virginia, Indiana, Kentucky, and Illinois.

rivers that flow into the Ohio. The region's location affects its climate. For much of the region, there are no mountains to the north or south. So, cold air comes down from the Arctic. Warm, humid air comes up from the Gulf of Mexico.

THE OHIO VALLEY

For this reason, the region can experience a wide range of temperatures. Winters can be extremely cold. Summers can become very hot. The southern states of Kentucky and Tennessee tend to be warmer. Illinois, Indiana, and Ohio are farther north. They tend to be colder. Northern Missouri is also colder. But the state's southern part is warmer.

West Virginia's climate is different from the rest of the region. The state's mountains are part of the reason why. Higher up, temperatures are cooler. This makes summers milder. West Virginia is also closer to the East Coast. The Atlantic Ocean brings humid air to the coast. As a result, parts of West Virginia receive large amounts of rain.

Other parts of the Ohio Valley have lots of precipitation, too. Illinois and Indiana both border Lake Michigan. Ohio touches Lake Erie. These lakes are part of the Great Lakes. They are huge bodies

THE FORT ANCIENT PEOPLE

People have lived in the Ohio Valley for thousands of years. One group was the Fort Ancient people. Some of them lived in northern Kentucky from 1300 to 1650. The people managed wild turkey populations and their habitat. They ate mostly male turkeys. That way, female turkeys continued to raise new young. It provided the group with a steady supply of food.

Parts of Indiana near Lake Michigan average more than 70 inches (178 cm) of snow each year.

of water. Areas near them often receive **lake-effect snow**. This is especially true to the south and east of the lakes.

Extreme weather happens throughout the Ohio Valley. Severe thunderstorms bring hail and high winds. They can bring large amounts of rainfall, too. The rain can lead to flash floods. Some storms can even form tornadoes.

CHAPTER 3

SERIOUS RISKS

Climate change is greatly affecting the Ohio Valley. Average temperatures are rising. As a result, heat waves are becoming more common. They are also getting more intense. Extreme heat is dangerous to people's health.

Heat waves can be especially harmful in cities. Cities are filled with sidewalks,

Chicago, Illinois, is a city with a high risk of extreme heat.

parking lots, streets, and buildings. These solid surfaces absorb heat. They make cities hotter than nearby natural areas. This is called the urban heat island effect.

Rising temperatures bring other changes. For instance, warmer air can hold more water vapor. That allows stronger storms to form. These storms can lead to major flooding.

Floods can have a variety of impacts. As with heat, cities can face extra risk. Cities are not covered by as much natural ground. Natural ground can often soak up water. But roads, sidewalks, and buildings do not. For this reason, floodwater can spread more easily through cities.

In 2016, West Virginia had historic flash floods. Strong waters carried cars far from where they'd been.

The landscape can also increase flood risk. Heavy rain can make rivers and streams overflow. Then flat areas near those rivers flood. These locations are called floodplains. Flooding is also a large risk in West Virginia. With its steep mountains, many people live in valleys. Heavy rain runs down the mountains. It can then flood low-lying areas.

Floods can also harm agriculture in the Ohio Valley. Winters and springs are warming especially fast. So, these seasons receive more extreme storms. As a result, there are worse floods in spring. This season is when farmers plant crops. However, floods can force farmers to plant later than usual. That can lead

PREDICTING A FLOOD

Hydrologists help predict flooding in an area. They measure the amount of water in a river, creek, or stream. Then, they look at how much rain is expected. They see if the soil can hold more water. Their findings are used in computer models. These models forecast if flooding will occur.

A 2022 drought dried up parts of the Mississippi River in Missouri.

to fewer crops or less production overall. Farmers can lose money as a result.

Lack of rain is also becoming more of a problem. Higher temperatures are one cause. On hotter days, more water evaporates. For this reason, droughts are becoming more intense, especially in the summer. Worse droughts also harm agriculture. That's because crops need water to grow.

LEO BERRY

Leo Berry wanted to help the environment. In 2021, the 11-year-old learned about a new bill in Indiana. Lawmakers planned to remove protection for the state's wetlands. Wetlands are areas of land that have a lot of moisture. They include marshes and swamps.

In response, Leo researched wetlands. He learned they are important resources. They can help prevent droughts and floods. They provide homes for fish, birds, and animals. Wetlands even help clean the water.

Leo learned that most of Indiana's wetlands were already gone. He believed people should protect the remaining ones. He did not want lawmakers to pass the bill. So, Leo took action. He created a **petition** to stop the bill. By the spring of 2021, more than 20,000 people had signed it.

Indiana is home to many kinds of wetlands, including bogs, swamps, and marshes.

The bill became a law in April 2021. However, Leo's actions had still helped. Lawmakers had made some changes. The law still weakened wetland protections. But it left more protections than the original bill did.

CHAPTER 4

CALL TO ACTION

People burn huge amounts of fossil fuels. Fossil fuels include oil, natural gas, and coal. They are formed from plants and animals that died long ago. Burning fossil fuels powers cars and trucks. It produces heat and electricity. But burning fossil fuels also releases **greenhouse gases**. Carbon dioxide is one

In 2021, coal produced approximately three-quarters of Missouri's electricity.

example. These gases are the main cause of climate change.

To slow climate change, people must burn far less fossil fuels. Changing how power is made is one step. For instance, all Ohio Valley states rely heavily on coal-fired power plants. West Virginia and Missouri burn the most coal. Natural gas plants are another source of fossil fuels. In the 2010s, Indiana and Ohio began using much more natural gas.

People can use other sources of energy instead of fossil fuels. Two main types are solar and wind power. These energy sources release far less greenhouse gases. Illinois is a leading US state for

By 2020, Illinois was making the fifth-most wind power of all US states.

wind power. Some cities are taking important steps, too. Cincinnati, Ohio, is one example. In 2022, a huge solar farm began providing power to the city. It helped the city release less greenhouse gases into the atmosphere.

Transportation is another area of focus. More people are shifting to electric vehicles. These vehicles do not run on gasoline. Instead, they use batteries charged by electricity. Electric vehicles produce less greenhouse gases.

Many Ohio Valley cities have switched to electric buses. Some cities use electric police cars. Electric garbage trucks and fire trucks are also available. Large trucks bring goods to the Ohio Valley. They burn diesel fuel. This fuel is a major carbon emitter. However, companies are building electric trucks. They can replace polluting diesel trucks.

Even with these steps, climate change will still affect the region. The Ohio Valley must also adapt to the climate crisis.

An electric car charges at a station in Chattanooga, Tennessee.

For example, cities can improve how they deal with heat waves. One way is called green infrastructure. Cities can plant more trees and shrubs. Some can even grow on rooftops. These steps help reduce the urban heat island effect.

Green infrastructure can also help with floods and droughts. For instance, some cities develop rain gardens. These gardens lie lower than paved surfaces. Stormwater drains into them. The gardens are filled with native plants. The plants soak up water. This helps prevent flooding. In addition, walls stop pollution

DOES A LAKE HAVE RIGHTS?

In August 2014, pollution created an algae bloom in Lake Erie. The toxic bloom harmed people in Toledo, Ohio. Their drinking water became unsafe. People in Toledo took action. They developed a "bill of rights" for the lake. The lake would have the right not to be polluted. In 2019, Toledo residents voted on the issue. They passed the bill. But in 2020, a judge ruled against it. Even so, other places are recognizing the rights of nature.

A park in Cleveland, Ohio, showcases its rain garden.

in the stormwater. That way, filtered water flows back into the water supply. Cities can use this water during droughts.

The dangers of climate change are affecting the Ohio Valley. However, people in the region are finding ways to slow the crisis and adapt.

FOCUS ON
THE OHIO VALLEY

Write your answers on a separate piece of paper.

1. Write a letter to a friend describing what you learned about Leo Berry.

2. What do you think are the most damaging effects of climate change in the Ohio Valley? Why?

3. What is an example of green infrastructure?
>   **A.** petitions
>   **B.** flash floods
>   **C.** rain gardens

4. Why would roads and sidewalks help floodwater spread more easily?
>   **A.** They let water soak in more quickly.
>   **B.** They soak in less water, so more water rushes along the ground.
>   **C.** They soak in more water, so the ground gets wetter faster.

Answer key on page 32.

GLOSSARY

climate change
A long-term change in Earth's temperature, air pressure, or wind patterns due to human activity or natural causes.

flash flood
A sudden rush of water caused by heavy rain.

flood stage
The height at which a body of water will overflow its banks and cause flooding.

greenhouse gases
Gases that trap heat in the atmosphere. Raising these gases' atmospheric levels can lead to climate change.

lake-effect snow
Heavy snow produced when a cold air mass travels over a warmer body of water.

petition
A formal request to an authority signed by many people.

precipitation
Water that falls from clouds to the ground. It can be in the form of rain, hail, or snow.

stream gauge
An instrument that measures a stream or river's water level.

TO LEARN MORE

BOOKS

Kehoe, Rachel. *Improving Farming and Food Science to Fight Climate Change*. Lake Elmo, MN: Focus Readers, 2023.

Kim, Carol. *Climate Change on the Brink*. North Mankato, MN: Capstone Press, 2022.

Saxton, Anna. *Ohio*. Minneapolis: Abdo Publishing, 2023.

NOTE TO EDUCATORS

Visit **www.focusreaders.com** to find lesson plans, activities, links, and other resources related to this title.

INDEX

Answer Key: **1.** Answers will vary; **2.** Answers will vary; **3.** C; **4.** B